# LOOSE ENDS

## RELEASING-REWIRING-RELOVING SIMPLIFIED

11 STAGES OF 11 LESSONS
IN 11 CHAPTERS

WordPlay Beauty

authorHOUSE®

*AuthorHouse™*
*1663 Liberty Drive*
*Bloomington, IN 47403*
*www.authorhouse.com*
*Phone: 833-262-8899*



*Published by AuthorHouse 12/21/2022*

*ISBN: 978-1-6655-7096-1 (sc)*
*ISBN: 978-1-6655-7095-4 (hc)*
*ISBN: 978-1-6655-7097-8 (e)*

*Library of Congress Control Number: 2022917150*

*Print information available on the last page.*

# CONTENTS

Dear Love,

I am apologizing for hurting you internally as well as externally. It hurts me so much to look at how beautiful you always were and still are but now it is more in depth, with more knowledge, wisdom, insight, mercy, grace, and experience. You were always worth saving and I know that I let you down quite a bit knowing how much pain you had already endured. Lifting you up and dragging you down.

I have known you your whole life and always admired the beauty and strength within you, but I continuously betrayed you.

I vividly remember holding you while you cried and prayed so many days and nights from a child to adulthood that no one knew about. You are the prize that I have always loved but sometimes I did not with knowingly allowed others to love you unproperly.

Healing from your own open wounds was going to be one of the hardest things that you ever had to do in your life, and I was going to be there with you every step of the way because it was no longer about anyone else.

I congratulate you abundantly because you put in the work despite the conflict, confusion, or circumstances as well as the viewpoint of others.

You are profound, prolific, intelligent, self-empowered and breathtakingly beautiful from the inside out.

No longer running from the things just purpose-fully walking threw everything that once frightened you and you will become successful in everything you put your hands and mind too from this day forward the obstacles placed before you are mere illusions that you are strong enough to dissipate.

So, embrace the new foundation of ordained love in love in your life and allow abundance, harmony, alignment and most importantly PEACE that you have earned flow freely within you.

I promise to never lose or betray you ever again as long as breath is in this body.

I FORGIVE ME WHOLEHEARTEDLY

LOVE, WordPlayBeauty

# DEDICATION

This book is dedicated to my HIGHER POWER, Ancestors, and My Beautiful Family that has supported thus far. Also the individuals that need my story to make their next move on their Soul FULL Journey.

Acts 8:27

"And he arose and went: and, behold, a man of Ethiopia, an eunuch of great authority under Candace queen of the Ethiopians, who had the charge of all her treasure, and had come to Jerusalem for worship."

# PREFACE

This book is based on my life of fire, water, air and earth and it came about after my whole life shifted and shattered in November 2019. Everything and everyone that I thought I knew had been a lie. To know what it is to no longer feel and become so numb to the pain that I broke in places that I never knew existed. That is when I discovered my truth, self-worth as well as my journey. It is an important part of the Journey to face myself and advocacies in order to get and stay on the path that YOU are being guided to pave.

FIRE-MY TURMOIL

WATER-MY TEARS

AIR-MY BREATHING

EARTH-MY PEACE

Thank you to the beautiful souls that I have connected with thus far, the good, bad, and indifferent.

# CHAPTER 1

## Blowing the Candles Out

The feelings of love, peace, abundance, and freedom are different from what we were trained to think they are. These were the first and last things that I had craved during the process of a divorce from a marriage and all things that tried to destroy me not only mentally but emotionally, financially, and spiritually.

So many times, I wanted to act a like fool, but I did not. I chose the opposite because my purpose requires me to constantly elevate but to fulfill my duty. Overall, I look back at how far I have come and the mercy and grace that was bestowed upon me during my process, and I refuse to miss opportunities by focusing on someone or situation that no longer fit in my life purpose or destiny.

It took some time to get adjusted to my transformation, but I did it because what I had experienced throughout my divorce but throughout my existence were things that prepared me for my beautiful purpose in this lifetime. My dreams for you all is to survive and supersede any obstacles that you may encounter or have encountered. This segment of my existence is bigger than me. My GOD has given me the go ahead to blow out the last candle that barely illuminated the dark room I had been trapped in for so many years. I did just that and blew it out. Now so much light illuminates the darkness that was once there. Here I stand as a tree of life, letting go of part me that I fought in order to gain the proper substance. My last chapter is my first.

I WAS MAPPING THIS OUT I HIT
THE HEIST BACKWARDS
-KING NIPSEY HUSTLE-

# CAPÍTULO 1

## Soplando las velas

Los sentimientos de amor, paz, abundancia y libertad son diferentes de lo que nos enseñaron a pensar que son. Estas fueron las primeras y últimas cosas que había anhelado durante el proceso de divorcio de un matrimonio y todas las cosas que intentaron destruirme no solo mental sino emocional, financiera y espiritualmente.

Tantas veces, quise actuar como un tonto, pero no lo hice. Elegí lo contrario porque mi propósito me exige elevarme constantemente pero cumplir con mi deber. En general, miro hacia atrás a lo lejos que he llegado y la misericordia y la gracia que se me otorgaron durante mi proceso, y me niego a perder oportunidades centrándome en alguien o situación que ya no encaja en el propósito o el destino de mi vida.

Me tomó un tiempo adaptarme a mi transformación, pero lo hice porque lo que había experimentado durante mi divorcio pero a lo largo de mi existencia fueron cosas que me prepararon para mi hermoso propósito en esta vida. Mi sueño para todos ustedes es sobrevivir y superar cualquier obstáculo que puedan encontrar o hayan encontrado. Este segmento de mi existencia es más grande que yo. Mi DIOS me ha dado el visto bueno para apagar la última vela que apenas iluminaba el cuarto oscuro en el que había estado atrapado durante tantos años. Hice exactamente eso y lo arruiné. Ahora tanta luz ilumina la oscuridad que una vez estuvo allí.

Aquí estoy como un árbol de la vida, dejando ir una parte de mí que luché para obtener la sustancia adecuada. Mi último capítulo es el primero.

ESTABA MAPEO DE ESTO, GOLPEÉ

EL ATRACO HACIA ATRÁS

-REY NIPSEY HUSTLE-

# CHAPTER 2

## (Judge) Ment

Leaving in July 2021 before the magistrate made her final judgement was ideal for me since I was barely at the residence.

I had given up everything that was obtained before and during the marriage being asked by multiple individuals why I would do such a thing.

All I wanted was my peace and I was fighting for it day in and day out. This question showed me that society valued things more than there mental and emotional stability.

Once I prayed on it, I received my answer as to why!

I would no longer need those things
because they did not comply or compliment
my life and who I really am.

My mind, body, and spirit had changed drastically.

As I was in transition, I was being harassed
physically and spiritually from a distance.

I had broken down my life and dealt with
myself, so the plots and spiritual manipulations
and the women and men who had been hired
to cause chaos and conflict in me and around
me were not as effective as my lesson and the
women and men that had been hired to cause
chaos and conflict in me and around me.

I continued to stay focused during that time
period with the help of my understanding. I

saw and learned so much about myself from the new individuals I had now connected with.

"There is currently 1 individual left from my past that I am in communication with and find peace in. They have always shown gratitude and appreciation toward me."

My slate was wiped completely clean of the old me, and I was honored to see who and what was against me as well as for me

I received the documents stating that I was officially divorced on an incredibly special day of a loved one's birthday, and the only thing I could do was cry uncontrollably. I was no longer tied to someone legally someone who's had broken so many laws physically as well as spiritually to make my new phase and others connected to my life chaotic or non-existent.

Although the magistrate had made the judgement in court my GOD had made the last judgement call for the un-ordained commitment that I had placed myself in.

It never dawned on me what the value- of organic Love was until I followed the voice of others and not the voice of GOD that I would have had to experience what was clearly and blindly called obsessive lust.

# ART-of-FACT:

The devil does not know your future only your past! So that is what keeps being shown to you through illusions to lower your frequency level and make you fall back to what individuals use to see and know. When you deal with you the correct way and actually do the healing work required for you to make it to the next phase of your existence, no one can stop you but you.

# -OVERCOMING YOUR JUDGEMENT-

Reassessing your own awareness will help you to find your place of contentment and help you move forward toward your victory without dwelling on what has occurred

1. Why do you need to reassess your awareness?

We must allow things to flow through us internally and then out of us externally for proper healing.

2. Speak out loud, write and conform the reason for you fighting for your individuality.

Be able to identify you are participating in any situation in your life.

3. Write down and be fully aware of your own judgement.

Accept and learn from that judgement that

was rendered with an open heart.

4. How are you going to accept what was?

Focus on who you want to become without confusion.

5. Are you going to accept your authenticity?

-Things you will need to get started-

YOU

YOUR SAVIOR

PRAYER

YOUR BELIEFS

FAITH

PEN and PAPER

# CHAPITRE 2

## (Judgement)

Partir en juillet 2021 avant que la magistrate ne rende son jugement définitif était idéal pour moi puisque j'étais à peine à la résidence. J'avais renoncé à tout ce qui avait été obtenu avant et pendant le mariage, étant demandé par plusieurs personnes pourquoi je ferais une telle chose.

Tout ce que je voulais, c'était ma paix et je me battais pour elle jour après jour. Cette question m'a montré que la société valorisait les choses plus que la stabilité mentale et émotionnelle. Une fois que j'ai prié dessus, j'ai reçu ma réponse quant au pourquoi !

Je n'aurais plus besoin de ces choses parce qu'elles ne se conformaient pas ou ne complimentaient pas ma vie et qui je suis vraiment. Mon esprit, mon corps et mon esprit avaient radicalement changé. Comme j'étais en transition, j'étais harcelée physiquement et spirituellement à distance.

J'avais brisé ma vie et m'étais occupé de moi-même, donc les complots et les manipulations spirituelles et les femmes et les hommes qui avaient été embauchés pour semer le chaos et les conflits en moi et autour de moi n'étaient pas aussi efficaces que ma leçon et les femmes et les hommes qui avaient été embauché pour semer le chaos et le conflit en moi et autour de moi. J'ai continué à rester concentré pendant cette période avec l'aide de ma compréhension. J'ai vu et appris tellement de choses sur moi-même grâce aux nouvelles personnes avec lesquelles j'étais désormais en contact. "Il reste actuellement une personne de mon passé avec qui je suis en communication et dans laquelle je trouve la paix. Ils m'ont toujours montré de la gratitude et de l'appréciation."

Mon ardoise a été complètement nettoyée de l'ancien moi, et j'ai été honoré de voir qui et ce qui était contre moi ainsi que pour moi J'ai reçu les documents indiquant que j'étais officiellement divorcé un jour incroyablement spécial de l'anniversaire d'un être cher, et la seule chose que je pouvais faire était de pleurer de manière incontrôlable. Je n'étais plus lié à quelqu'un légalement quelqu'un qui avait enfreint tant de lois physiquement et spirituellement pour rendre ma nouvelle phase et d'autres liées à ma vie chaotiques ou inexistantes. Bien que le magistrat ait rendu le jugement au tribunal, mon DIEU avait prononcé le dernier jugement pour l'engagement non ordonné dans lequel je m'étais placé. Il ne m'est jamais venu à l'esprit quelle était la valeur de l'amour organique jusqu'à ce que je suive la voix des autres et non la voix de DIEU que j'aurais dû expérimenter ce qui était clairement et aveuglément appelé luxure obsessionnelle.

# ART-de-FACT:

Le diable ne connaît pas votre avenir que votre passé ! C'est donc ce qui ne cesse de vous être montré à travers des illusions pour abaisser votre niveau de fréquence et vous faire retomber sur ce que les individus utilisent pour voir et savoir. Lorsque vous traitez avec vous de la bonne manière et que vous effectuez réellement le travail de guérison nécessaire pour passer à la phase suivante de votre existence, personne ne peut vous arrêter à part vous.

# - SURMONTER VOTRE JUGEMENT-

Réévaluer votre propre conscience vous aidera à trouver votre lieu de contentement et vous aidera à avancer vers votre victoire sans vous attarder sur ce qui s'est passé

1. Pourquoi avez-vous besoin de réévaluer votre conscience ?

Nous devons permettre aux choses de s'écouler à travers nous à l'intérieur puis à l'extérieur de nous pour une bonne guérison.

2. Parlez à haute voix, écrivez et conformez la raison pour laquelle vous vous battez pour votre individualité.

Soyez capable d'identifier que vous participez à n'importe quelle situation de votre vie.

3. Écrivez et soyez pleinement conscient de votre propre jugement.

Acceptez et apprenez de ce jugement qui a été rendu avec un cœur ouvert.

4 Comment allez-vous accepter ce qui était ? Concentrez-vous sur qui vous voulez devenir sans confusion.

5. Allez-vous accepter votre authenticité ?

-Les choses dont vous aurez besoin pour commencer-

TU

VOTRE

SAUVEUR

PRIÈRE

VOS CROYANCES

FOI

Stylo et papier

# CHAPTER 3

## Hoax or a {Hex}

It was on the twenty-first day of April 2018 that everything shifted tremendously from the inside for me. I found out that I had been a complete catalyst for the individuals that were paid and some just willingly because they were sleeping with my (ex). Perpetrators I had came up against me, all because I was starting a new life.

The Haitian Hexes' were being thrown full force at me and every aspect of my life around the clock until his money ran out and he owed those practitioners.

When I looked back from day one to November 2019, when I was served twice with divorce papers, I realize I had been set up for murder. It was all a game from the beginning with him and his friends and lovers.

I was dancing with the devil himself,
and I knew it but others didn't until some
witnessed what was being done to me.

I had been under a veil of lies the entire time and
then it was revealed to me what had been going on.

I had uncovered secrets about the people who
said they loved me once upon a time, but they
wanted their secrets to stay as secrets and they
tried any and everything necessary to keep
the addictions, sexual escapes, secret children,
money frauds, and other things private.

I told quite a few "-so-called-" friends and family
members about this and some looked at me as if
I was crazy, and others looked at me like this is
what you get because they never cared anyway.

The memories flowed through my mind clearly and vividly:. There was drinking, and kickbacks. There were vacations where I would drink and wake up with not remembering anything I mean nothing. But where it would seem that I had had sex without protection but when I would ask, the answer would be no. As if I didn't know my own body. And then my things would be missing from the house. But with just us in the residence, that made no sense, but I guess I was delusional and had no idea how to properly function after being hexed for so long.

I swept a whole continent under the rug willingly and unwillingly while trying to give love to a lifeless structure; some days I could not move or think.

Until I was forced to sit still and look at everything and everyone around me. I had no choice but to figure out what my life was prior to this, as well as what it is going to be or become a victim of my circumstances and seeing what was done to me.

As I sat with myself, I knew me enough to understand that the way my behavior kept changing was not me. That is how I figured out how far back this betrayal had started. If I prayed and stay connected to the higher ups, I would not lose my faith. And I was not I willing to lose my sanity over someone else's beliefs, underlining childhood issues, greed, or public reputation.

Still surrounded by everything that was going on, I would often become slightly sick. My money was affected no matter how hard I worked on projects as well as how many hours I put in. I discovered who kept placing hexs' on me in every aspect of my life.

It was to the point that I was being followed by different individuals as well as private investigators.

They would send different individuals to try and sleep with me as well as project their negative energy on to me or demonic energy on-to me.

I kept my head held high and fought for that little girl inside of me consistently. I was the protection that she needed while growing up. You would have never known that I was experiencing so many adversities in my circumstances by the way I looked and kept moving forward all because I knew who I was and who I was connected to. I have the guidance in my soul and heart.

# ART-of-FACT

When others begin to dabble into the evil sides of the realm to stop you or hinder your progression in life that is when you know that you are more powerful and valuable then what you realize. When you are shown a group of individuals trying to stop you because a relationship failed, keep moving forward no matter how hard it gets. Always remember you are never alone.

During my isolation I had to decipher the patterns to figure out this puzzle of illusions and learning to not sit in my thoughts and overthink what I was seeing and what I knew as fact.

One would have thought that we could have peacefully resolved the divorce process and gone on with our lives but the individuals that he paid to do hexing's on me had also done it on the attorneys as well as the judge for the court case to go in his favor.

I figured that out when everyone would just walk around happy and smiling and no documented was ever turned in on time or if at all prior to our court dates. The documents that were turned in were modified by his friends to make it look legit and I would bring it up in court with my attorney as well as his attorney and the only thing I received was a continuance from March of 2020-Dec of 2021 with the only thing being needed was an accurate appraisal.

What was being done to me behind closed doors was brutal and I would not wish on anyone, for individuals to stoop so low to try and unalive you threw the form of HEX's to make it seem like one has transitioned naturally is disturbing and unbearable for material gain and humanities notoriety is scary but very real,

You have people selling their souls, obtaining false God complexes, and thinking that they are bigger, mightier, and stronger than GOD, but they will be made a mockery out of because they are mocking GOD aimlessly and misleading the masses with their illusions.

"You cannot destroy what you did not create"

# HELP & KEY NOTES

1. Ask yourself what and who has caused you to become the person that you are?

2. What are you going to do with the truth after realization?

3. Are you going to let yourself heal from what you have discovered or point the finger at the people that have caused you pain?

One thing that I noticed when I was dealing with the exposure of spell work the underlying purpose is to destroy you as a being, F.E.A.R and isolation is what is commonly projected on to you so that you can't release yourself from hardships or traumas that you have experienced throughout life or failed relationships and to focus on what is being done to you and not for you will weaken your defense so now the work is actually penetrating you and you're feeling the full effect of it.

The key is knowing the difference between your energy and others energy. Being aware of specific things while you are in isolation will give you more insight of who you are as well as what you feel from within.

During that period, I had created my future visually and started working towards it physically.

I did have a few setbacks/restarts as I continued because of the projections and spells where still happening, had I not been a victim of witchcraft I would have never really believed the horrible things that society does in order to stop someone's destiny, freewill and abundant birth right.

So be very mindful of who and what you focus on as well as what you spend your time on physically, spiritually, and visually.

# פרק 3

# {Hex} או מתיחה

שהכל 2018 באפריל ואחד העשרים ביום היה זה עבור מוחלט זרז שהייתי גיליתי .עבורי מבפנים מאוד השתנה האקס) עם שכבו הם כי מרצון רק וחלקם שכר שקיבלו האנשים חיים שהתחלתי בגלל הכל ,בי נתקלו לי שהיו עבריינים .(שלי מסביב בחיי היבט כל ועל עליי נזרקו האיטיים המשושים .חדשים האלה למתרגלים חייב היה והוא שלו הכסף שנגמר עד ,לשעון כאשר ,201 לנובמבר הראשון מהיום אחורה כשהסתכלתי .לרצח שהוכננתי מבינה אני ,גירושין תעודות פעמיים לי הוגשו עם רקדתי .ואוהביו חבריו ועם איתו מההתחלה משחק היה הכל עדים היו שחלקם עד לא אחרים אבל זה את וידעתי ,עצמו השטן ואז הזמן כל שקרים של מעטה תחת הייתי .לי שעושים למה שהם שאמרו האנשים על סודות חשפתי .קרה מה לי התגלה כסודות יישארו שלהם שהסודות רצו הם אבל ,פעם אותי אהבו

בריחות ,ההתמכרויות על לשמור כדי שצריך מה כל ניסו והם

פְּרָטִי .אחרים דברים ועוד כסף הונאות ,סודיים ילדים ,מיניות

"-שנקרא מה-" משפחה ובני חברים מעט ללא זה על סיפרתי

עליי הסתכלו ואחרים ,משוגע אני כאילו עליי הסתכלו וחלקם

.אכפת להם היה לא ממילא כי מקבל שאתה מה זה כאילו

,שתייה הייתה ..וחיה ברורה בצורה במוחי זרמו הזיכרונות

לזכור בלי ומתעוררת שותה הייתי שבהן חופשות היו .ועיטות

יחסי שקיימתי שנראה איפה אבל .לכלום מתכוונת לא אני כלום

לא כאילו .לא תהיה התשובה ,שואל כשהייתי אבל הגנה ללא מין

אבל .מהבית חסרים יהיו שלי הדברים ואז .שלי הגוף את הכרתי

שהייתי מניח אני אבל ,הגיוני היה לא זה ,במעון אנחנו כשרק

משוחק שהייתי אחרי כראוי לתפקד איך מושג לי היה ולא הוזה

ברצון לשטיח מתחת שלמה יבשת טטאתי .זמן הרבה כך כל

כמה ;חיים חסר למבנה אהבה להעניק ניסיון תוך רצון ובחוסר

בשקט לשבת שנאלצתי עד .לחשוב או לזוז יכולתי לא ימים

אלא ברירה לי הייתה לא .שסביבי מי כל ועל הכל על ולהסתכל

להיות הולכים הם מה גם כמו ,זה לפני שלי החיים היו מה להבין

לי נעשה מה ולראות שלי הנסיבות של לקורבן להפוך או.

שבה שהדרך להבין כדי מספיק אותי הכרתי ,עצמי עם כשישבתי

הבגידה כמה עד הבנתי כך .אני לא היא השתנתה שלי ההתנהגות

לא ,לגבוהים מחובר ואשאר מתפלל הייתי אם .התחילה הזו

שלי השפיות להפסיד מוכן הייתי ולא .שלי האמונה את אאבד

ילדות בעיות הדגשת תוך ,אחר מישהו של לאמונות ביחס,

לעתים ,שקורה מה בכל מוקף עדיין .ציבורי מוניטין או חמדנות

קשה כמה משנה לא הושפע שלי הכסף .מעט חולה הייתי קרובות

מי גיליתי .השקעתי שעות כמה גם כמו ,פרויקטים על עבדתי

כך כדי עד היה זה .חיי של היבט בכל קסם עלי להטיל המשיך

היו הם .פרטיים חוקרים גם כמו שונים אנשים אחרי שעקבו

את להקרין גם כמו ,איתי ולשכב לנסות שונים אנשים שולחים

עליי הדמונית האנרגיה את או עליי שלהם השלילית האנרגיה.

שבתוכי הקטנה הילדה עבור ונלחמתי גבוה ראשי את הרמתי

שגדלתי בזמן לה זקוקה הייתה שהיא ההגנה הייתי .בעקביות

בנסיבות מצוקות הרבה כך כל חווה שאני יודע היית לא לעולם

אני מי ידעתי כי הכל להתקדם והמשכתי שנראיתי איך לפי ,שלי

ובלב בנשמה ההדרכה את לי יש .מחובר אני ולמי

# ART-of-FACT

לצדדים להתעסק מתחילים כשאחרים

ההתקדמות את לעכב או אותך לעצור כדי הממלכה של הרעים

ממה יותר ערך ובעל חזק שאתה יודע אתה כאשר זה ,בחיים שלך

לעצור שמנסים אנשים של קבוצה לך כשמראים .מבין שאתה

משנה לא להתקדם המשיכי ,נכשלה יחסים שמערכת בגלל אותך

במהלך .לבד לא פעם אף שאתה תמיד זכור .יהיה זה קשה כמה

חידת את להבין כדי הדפוסים את לפענח נאלצתי שלי הבידוד

מדי יותר ולחשוב שלי במחשבות לשבת לא וללמוד הזו האשליות

לחשוב היה אפשר .כעובדה שידעתי ומה רואה שאני מה על

ולהמשיך שלום בדרכי הגירושין הליך את לפתור יכולים שהיינו

עשו הקסם עליי לעשות כדי שילם שהוא האנשים אבל ,בחיינו

המשפט בית שתיק כדי השופט על וגם הדין עורכי על גם זאת

שמחים יסתובבו פשוט כשכולם זה את הבנתי .טוֹבָה יעבור

תאריכי לפני בכלל אם או בזמן הוגש לא מסמך ואף ומחייכים

כדי חבריו ידי על שונו שהוגשו המסמכים .שלנו המשפט בית

עורך עם המשפט בבית זה את מעלה והייתי לגיטימי ייראה שזה

היה שקיבלתי היחיד והדבר שלו הדין עורך עם וגם שלי הדין

שהיה היחיד הדבר עם 2021 דצמבר עד 2020 ממרץ המשך

היה סגורות בדלתיים לי שנעשה מה .מדויקת הערכה היה צריך

אחד לאף מאחל הייתי ולא אכזרי

# CHAPTER 4

## Self-Inflicted Wounds (Mirrored Reflections)

I had been snapped in half, with nothing left to grasp onto besides my heart and my hurt as I laid on the floor in fetal position. Disregarding my intuition is what prompted me to experience the changes in my life, fully giving me the biggest humbling of my existence by listening to what was outside of me instead of what I really felt on the inside. Realizing I had cheated myself out of many years of happiness. Not just with the marriage but with every other relationship I had formed. That is what most do and due to me not being healed I did not know how to value all aspects of my life properly.

# THE TREE HAD FALLING

That is when the unwrapping "healing" started. I had to re nurture myself from childbirth to adulthood to obtain the correct insight, I started to dig and broke the first shovel and wanted to stop because a lot of it hurt terribly and at times it was unbearable because I became more aware of who I was not. I continued to dig breaking many shovels to get to the root of the major lesson I was experiencing.

The clear sense and clarity that I had obtained Wow digging is that I have been longing for what happened inside of me the whole time and that was true love, I did not know how to bring it out for myself and willingly brought it out and flooded everyone else that I had ever encountered in this life. because I was immune and traumatized by the mistreatment and manipulation of others, I continuously sacrificed my value. Not only did I realize how much others had manipulated my being, I also took accountability for how much I had manipulated myself by not being aware of what it was being poured on me by others. I did as I was shown during my meditation and I took my love, loyalty and place it up on the little girl inside of me that needed it and deserved it the most.

Being broken down from your root had become a beautiful reflection, although at times I was afraid and I did not want to face certain events that had occurred, GOD and I were the fuel to make it over the hurdles that I continuously fell over without knowing why until I completely surrendered. Going through my transformation I would often sit and cry because I was actually falling in love for the first time in my life and it was not with someone outside of me. I cry for my past, present and future because my heart and soul were finally free with no confusion or attachments, I had found the right key to put in the door to my HOME

# ART-OF-FACT

Slowing down at times to take in the beauty of your experiences can help you rewire your thinking and show the true effects of healing PIECE by (PEACE), serving YOURSELF kindness and T(RUTH).

# HELP & KEY NOTES

How do you think you went wrong?

Ask yourself what went wrong?

Why do you believe you are not worthy?

Not why everyone else feels their way!

Revelation 4:11

# ƆнɒQʇɘɿ M

## ƧɘlʇIᴎʇlicʇɘb Wounbƨ Miɿɿoɿɘb Яɘʇlɘcʇionƨ

I нɒb dɘɘn ƨnɒqqɘb in нɒlʇ wiʇн noʇнinϱ lɘʇʇ ʇo
ϱɿɒƨq onʇo dɘƨibɘƨ my нɘɒɿʇ ɒnb my нuɿʇ ɒƨ I lɒib on
ʇнɘ ɿooʇ in ʇɘʇɒl qoƨiʇionᗡiƨɿɘϱɒɿbinϱ my inʇuiʇion
iƨ wнɒʇ qɿomqʇɘb mɘ ʇo ɘxqɘɿiɘncɘ ʇнɘ ɔнɒnϱɘƨ
in my liʇɘ ʇully ϱivinϱ mɘ ʇнɘ diϱϱɘƨʇ нumdlinϱ
oʇ my ɘxiƨʇɘncɘ dy liƨʇɘninϱ ʇo wнɒʇ wɒƨ ouʇƨibɘ
oʇ mɘ inƨʇɘɒb oʇ wнɒʇ I ɿɘɒlly ʇɘlʇ on ʇнɘ inƨibɘЯ
ɘɒlizinϱ I нɒb ɔнɘɒʇɘb myƨɘlʇ ouʇ oʇ mɒny yɘɒɿƨ
oʇ нɒqqinɘƨƨ Noʇ juƨʇ wiʇн ʇнɘ mɒɿɿiɒϱɘ duʇ wiʇн
ɘvɘɿy oʇнɘɿ ɿɘlɒʇionƨнiq I нɒb ʇoɿmɘb Tнɒʇ iƨ wнɒʇ
moƨʇ bo ɒnb buɘ ʇo mɘ noʇ dɘinϱ нɘɒlɘb I bib noʇ
ʞnow нow ʇo vɒluɘ ɒll ɒƨqɘcʇƨ oʇ my liʇɘ qɿoqɘɿly

## THƎ TЯƎƎ HAꓷ ⸗ALLIИG

Tнɒɟ is wнen ɟнe unwɿɒpping нeɒling sɟɒɿɟeb

I нɒb ɟo ɿe nuɿɟuɿe myselɟ ɟɿom ɔнildbiɿɟн ɟo

ɒbulɟнoob ɟo obɟɒin ɟнe ɔoɿɿeɔɟ insiɡнɟ I sɟɒɿɟeb

ɟo biɡ ɒnb bɿoke ɟнe ɟiɿsɟ sнovel ɒnb wɒnɟeb

ɟo sɟoq beɔɒuse ɒ loɟ oɟ iɟ нuɿɟ ɟeɿɿibly ɒnb

ɒɟ ɟimes iɟ wɒs unbeɒɿɒble beɔɒuse I ɔɒme

moɿe ɒwɒɿe oɟ wнo I wɒs noɟ I ɔonɟinueb ɟo biɡ

bɿeɒkinɡ mɒny sнovels ɟo ɡeɟ ɟo ɟнe ɿooɟ oɟ ɟнe

mɒjoɿ lesson I wɒs expeɿienɔinɡTнe ɔleɒɿ sense

ɒnb ɔlɒɿiɟy ɟнɒɟ I нɒb obɟɒineb Wow biɡɡinɡ

is ɟнɒɟ I нɒve been lonɡinɡ ɟoɿ wнɒɟ нɒppeneb

insibe oɟ me ɟнe wнole ɟime ɒnb ɟнɒɟ wɒs ɟɿue

love I bib noɟ know нow ɟo bɿinɡ iɟ ouɟ ɟoɿ

myselɟ ɒnb willinɡly bɿouɡнɟ iɟ ouɟ ɒnb ɟeebeb

eveɿyone else ɟнɒɟ I нɒb eveɿ enɔounɟeɿeb in ɟнis

liɟe beɔɒuse I wɒs immune ɒnb ɟɿɒumɒɟizeb by

ɟнe misɟɿeɒɟmenɟ ɒnb mɒnipulɒɟion oɟ oɟнeɿs I

ɔonɟinuouƨly ƨɒɔɿiɟiɔəb my vɒluəNoɟ only bib I

ɿəɒlizə ʜow mɒɔʜ oɟʜəɿƨ ʜɒb mɒniqulɒɟəb my

ʜɔɒm woʜ ɿoɟ yɟiliɓɒɟnɒoɔɔɒ ʞooɟ oƨlɒ I ϱiəɓb → ɓnioϱ

I ʜɒb mɒniqulɒɟəb myƨəlɟ ɓy noɟ ɓniəϱ ɒwɒɿə

oɟ wʜɒɟ iɟ wɒƨ ɓniəϱ qoɒɿəb on mə ɓy oɟʜəɿƨ I

bib ɒƨ I wɒƨ ƨʜown bɒɿinϱ my məbiɟɒɟion ɒnb I

ɟooʞ my lovə loyɒlɟy ɒnb qlɒəɔ iɟ ɒq on ɟʜə liɟɟlə

bəvɿəƨəb ɒnb iɟ bəəbəəb ɟʜɒɟ əm ɟo əbiƨni lɿiϱ

iɟ ɟʜə moƨɟ ɓniəϱ bɿoʞən bown ɟɿom youɿ ɿooɟ

ʜɒb bəɔomə ɒ bəɒuɟiɟul ɿəɟləɔɟion ɒlɟʜouϱʜ ɒɟ

ɟimə ƨ I wɒƨ ɒɟɿɒib ɒnb I bib noɟ wɒnɟ ɟo ɟɒɔə

əɔɿɟɒin əvənɟƨ ɟʜɒɟ ʜɒb bəɔɒuɿɿəb ЭOG ɒnb I

wəɿə ɟʜə ɟuəl ɟo mɒʞə iɟ ovəɿ ɟʜə ʜuɿbləƨ ɟʜɒɟ

I ɔonɟinuouƨly ɟəll ovəɿ wiɟʜouɟ ʞnowinϱ wʜy

unɟil I ɔomqləɟəly ƨuɿɿənbəɿəb ϱoinϱ ɟʜɿouϱʜ

my ɟɿɒnƨɟoɿmɒɟion I woulb oɟɟən ƨiɟ ɒnb ɔɿy

bəɔɒuƨə I wɒƨ ɒɔɟuɒlly ɟɒllinϱ in lovə ɟoɿ ɟʜə

ɟiɿƨɟ ɟimə in my liɟə ɒnb iɟ wɒƨ noɟ wiɟʜ ƨoməonə

outside to me I cry for my past present and future

because my heart and soul were finally free

with no confusion or attachments I had found

the right key to put in the door to my HOME

# AЯTO⫤ ⫤AƆT

Ƨlowinϱ bown ɒɟ ɟimeƨ ɟo ɟɒʞe in ɟнe deɒuɟy oɟ

γoυ˥ əxqəʅiənɔəƨ ɔɒn нəlp γoυ ʅəwiʅə γoυ˥ ɟнinʞinϱ

ɒnb ƨнow ɟнə ɟʅυə əɟɟəɔɟƨ oɟ нəɒlinϱ ꟼIƎƆƎ dγ

ꟼƎAƆƎ ƨəʅvinϱ YOUЯƧƎ⅃⫤ ʞinbnəƨƨ ɒnbTЯUTH

# HƎ⅃ꟼ ꓘƎY NOTƎƧ

Where bo γou Ɉhinʞ γou wənɈ wɿonǫ?

Aƨʞ γouɿƨelɟ whɒɈ wenɈ wɿonǫ?

Whγ bo γou dəlievə γou ɒɿə noɈ woɿɈhγ?

ИoɈ whγ əvəɿγonə əlƨə ɟəəlƨ Ɉhəiɿ

wɒγЯəvəlɒɈion µll

# CHAPTER 5

## The Torn Pages

Implanted were red flags with bells and
whistles following closely behind that I
never missed but simply dismissed.
We all dismiss things when we see them
through the eyes in the world but not
of the WORLD "spiritual eyes."
Looking through society's, friends, or family eyes
can dictate what is best for us from there viewpoint.
Now expressing what was torn pages of my
life by not neglecting what was before me.

When I realized that the person, I decided to
commit myself to had many attached spirits
on them I had already made myself a blind

participant thinking because I had so much love
to give that I could help change the dynamic.
I was wrong and I knew that I was for trying
to do things threw the talks of others.

With everything going on inside of me
and on the outside, I knew “instinctively’
that what I was doing was a mistake.

# ART-OF-FACT

The lies were more consistent than

any other part of the lesson

# NON-ORDAINMENT

During the proposal my aunt's ponytail
fell right out of her head "distraction"
Down on one knew and the ring fell
to the ground "distraction"
Everyone started clapping saying that she
said "yes" when I did not give an answer
I said "Yes" but was not excited at all while everyone
went out and celebrated, I went to bed afterwards
I did not want to come out when the
time came to walk down the aisle
The pastor that married "supposedly" had
married us did not have the proper license. When
informed with that information a couple of
weeks later you would have thought that I would
have run for the hills "right' wrong we went to
the courthouse and got married properly.

The mask fell off

No emotional, mental, physical, financial support.
I pretty sure that I had put on the best show
for the outer world to see by forcing myself
to fall in love with someone and something
that didn't know how or what LOVE was.

I had found multiple phones, hidden under
the spare tires in the car and closets. I had no
idea that I had married a full-blown Narcissist.
I did not know the name of someone that
had all of the patterns and personalities.
Later finding out that I was being talked down on
continuously to the ones that I considered family
before the marriage, it was so many lies, and rumors
being spoken I just stopped talking because there was
no way that someone could falsify so many personas.
When I saw my life changing drastically, I
had to up my faith because I noticed that I was

being slowly stripped of my entire character.
He was pushing onto me who he really was,

and he wanted to become who I truly was. The way that my GOD is set-up, it was not allowed the only thing that was allowed was an exit strategy and if I was willing to take it.

# KEY & HELP NOTES

If someone does not talk with you but
talks about you two others terminate the
situation in any form of relationship.
if someone continuously talks about their
family and their friends in a negative
way or tone terminate the situation.
If your intuition, it is telling you that something
is not right terminate the situation.
Write down any key points in your journal
that you believe can help you in your
REALTY to recognize red flags.

# 第５章

## 引き裂かれたページ

植え付けられたのは、私が見逃すことはなく、単に却下されたすぐ後ろに続くベルとホイッスルを備えた赤旗でした。 世界の目を通してではなく、世界の「霊の目」を通して物事を見るとき、私たちは皆、物事を却下します。 社会、友人、または家族の目を通して見ることは、その観点から私たちにとって何が最善であるかを決定することができます. 今、目の前にあるものを無視しないことで、私の人生の引き裂かれたページを表現しています.

その人に気づいたとき、私は彼らに多くのスピリットが付着していることに専念することにしました。

私は間違っていました、そして、私は物事をやろうとしていることが他の人の話を投げかけたことを知っていました.

自分の内側と外側ですべてが起こっているので、自分のしていることは間違いだと「本能的に」わかりました。アート・オブ・ファクト 嘘はレッスンの他のどの部分よりも一貫していた

非叙階

プロポーズの最中、叔母のポニーテールが頭から抜け落ちた「気晴らし」

ダウンオンオン 知っていて、リングが地面に落ちた「気晴らし」 私が答えなかったとき、彼女が「はい」と言ったとみんなが拍手し始めま

した 私は「はい」と言いましたが、みんなが出かけてお祝いをしている間、まったく興奮せず、私はその後寝ました 通路を歩く時が来ても出たくなかった 「おそらく」私たちと結婚した牧師は、適切な免許を持っていませんでした。数週間後にその情報を知らされたとき、あなたは私が丘に向かって走っていただろうと思ったでしょう。

私たちは裁判所に行き、きちんと結婚しました. マスクが落ちた 感情的、精神的、肉体

的、精神的、経済的サポートはありません。私は、愛がどのように、または何であるかを知らなかった誰かや何かに恋をするように強制することで、外の世界が見るのに最高のショーをしたと確信しています。車やクローゼットのスペアタイヤの下に隠された複数の電話を見つけました。本格的なナルシストと結婚したとは思いもしませんでした。すべてのパターンと性格を持っている人の名前を知りませんでした。後になって、結婚前から家族だと思っていた人たちに、私が絶えず見下されていたことを知りました。それは嘘が多く、噂が流れていたので、私は話すのをやめました。自分の人生が劇的に変化するのを見たとき、自分の性格全体がゆっくりと剥奪されていることに気づいたので、信仰を強めなければなりませんでした。彼は本当の自分を私に押し付けていました。そして彼は私が本当の自分になりたがっていました。

私のGODが設定されている方法では、許されなかった唯一のことは出口戦略であり、私がそれを受け入れる意思があるかどうかでした.

キー＆ヘルプノート 誰かがあなたと話すのではなく、あなたのことを話すと、他の2人がどんな形の関係でもその状況を終わらせます。誰かが家族や友人について否定的な方法や口調で継続的に話している場合、状況を終わらせます. あなたの直観は、何かが正しくないことをあなたに伝えているのです。

REALTY で危険信号を認識するのに役立つと思われる重要なポイントを日記に書き留めてください。

# CHAPTER 6

## The Sun and the Shade

For those of you that do not know what gas lighting means here lies a brief description: It is a form of manipulation, an emotional abuse tactic where someone mentally misleads you creating a false narrative and making you question your own judgment and reality.

The honeymoon phase can seem like the fourth of July or the forest fires in California

I choose the forest fires in California because I thought that I knew what happiness and love was, so it was a slow painful burn I did not recognize.

2013 was my first year of freedom where I strictly saw sunshine and new beginnings for myself because that was my clean slate since I had just moved to a new state. I ran across a few hick-ups, but I remained focus until I got completely on my feet. Then I ran into the reason for the writing of my book.

Because I did not move fast with the situation that I placed myself in but when faced to look back I had knocked myself off of my pedestal when I decided to do something that I had never done before which was build an adult.

My perception of a relationship was presented to me in the form of a lust disguised love.

# ART-OF-FACT

The devil would have never had any way of maneuvering in my life had I not told what I wanted verses them showing me what I deserved as well as true character and intentions.

# -REGULATIONS-

You cannot fix nor change another individual if

they see nothing wrong with their behavior.

Do not disregard your true feelings and

what your spirit is SIGNALNG to you.

What work have you done to fix apart of

you that you are trying to fix in others?

How do you REALLY want to be treated?

# CAPITOLUL 6

## Soarele și Umbra

Pentru cei dintre voi care nu știu ce înseamnă iluminatul cu gaz, aici se află o scurtă descriere: este o formă de manipulare, o tactică de abuz emoțional în care cineva vă induce în eroare mental creând o narațiune falsă și făcându-vă să vă puneți la îndoială propria judecată și realitate.

Faza lunii de miere poate părea ca 4 iulie
sau incendiile forestiere din California

Aleg incendiile de pădure din California pentru că am crezut că știu ce este fericirea și dragostea, așa că a fost o arsură lentă și dureroasă pe care nu o recunoșteam. 2013 a fost primul meu an de libertate în care am văzut cu strictețe soare și noi începuturi pentru mine, pentru că asta a fost tabloul meu curat de când tocmai mă mutasem într-o nouă stare. Am alergat peste câteva scăpări, dar am rămas concentrat până m-am pus complet pe picioare. Apoi am dat de motivul pentru care am scris cartea.

Pentru că nu m-am mișcat repede cu situația în care m-am plasat, dar când m-am confruntat să privesc în urmă, m-am dat jos de pe piedestal, când am decis să fac ceva ce nu făcusem niciodată până acum, și anume să construiesc un adult. Percepția mea despre o relație mi-a fost prezentată sub forma unei iubiri deghizate de poftă.

# ARTA DE FAPT

Diavolul n-ar fi avut niciodată vreun fel de manevră în viața mea dacă nu mi-aş fi spus ce vreau, iar ele arătându-mi ceea ce merit, precum și adevăratul caracter și intențiile.

# -REGULI-

Nu puteți repara sau schimba un alt individ dacă

nu vede nimic rău în comportamentul său.

Nu neglijați adevăratele voastre sentimente și

ceea ce vă reprezintă spiritul SEMNAL.

Ce muncă ai făcut pentru a te despărți de tine

pe care încerci să le repari în ceilalți?

Cum vrei cu adevărat să fii tratat?

# CHAPTER 7

## Raw Emotions

Bringing forth lower-level emotions that I never knew how to transmute showed me my truth. I never knew that holding in all of your pain and disturbances could dictate your life so much so that it affects every choice that each and every one of us makes in life. Not knowing how to get over the traumas and near misses in everyday life by simply just existing. Those emotions turning into devastation and desperation to belong anywhere but inside of oneself, now caught in a ball of suffering thinking that you are actually having the time of your life, when you should be finding your true life to live in.

Expressing myself mildly instead of defensively I finally understood the translations of wounds, words, and feelings.

I know that pain is a heavy topic that no one wants to discuss or handle in the proper way because of what they have internalized and not wanting to relate or relive the moments but being more understanding with yourself and realizing the things that I had to endure were things that I had to master in order to teach other individuals about the lessons that I had to learn.

# ART-OF-FACT

Lessons prepare us for the future and are essential keys to doors that are closed.

Harboring these emotions that are not properly felt damages the true character of many.

Yearning for the answers of why something happened to me is the normalcy of society, it is just like saying "HELLO", instead of going within and praying or meditating on the situation to get the truth and the real identity of why something has transpired.

Once I stopped talking to myself and started speaking to myself, I saw things and heard things more clearly. Notice when you are talking to yourself, you are going to stay consistent with lying to yourself but when you are speaking to yourself you are more firm, sound, and clear on your boundaries that brings about that change you're searching for in order to get over the raw emotions of WHY me.

# RAW-QUESTION-AIR

How many opportunities have you missed
because of unfiltered emotions?
How many potential relationships have
you unknowingly removed from your life
because of those unfiltered emotions?
How captivating would it be to
YOU to finally be free?
Are you willing to dig for your recovery?
Are you willing to live in your truth
or (LIE) out your truth?

# SURA YA 7

# HISIA MBICHI

Kuleta hisia za kiwango cha chini ambazo sikuwahi kujua jinsi ya kuzibadilisha kulinionyesha ukweli wangu. Sikuwahi kujua kuwa kushikilia maumivu na usumbufu wako wote kunaweza kuamuru maisha yako hivi kwamba inaathiri kila chaguo ambalo kila mmoja wetu hufanya maishani.

Kutojua jinsi ya kukabiliana na kiwewe na misses karibu katika maisha ya kila siku kwa kuwepo tu. Hisia hizo zinazogeuka kuwa uharibifu na kukata tamaa kuwa mali popote lakini ndani yako mwenyewe, sasa umeshikwa na mpira wa mateso ukifikiri kwamba una wakati wa maisha yako, wakati unapaswa kutafuta maisha yako ya kweli ya kuishi.

Kujieleza kwa upole badala ya kujitetea hatimaye
nilielewa tafsiri za majeraha, maneno, na hisia.

Najua maumivu ni mada nzito ambayo hakuna
anayetaka kuijadili au kuishughulikia kwa njia
ipasavyo kwa sababu ya yale waliyoyaweka
ndani na sio kutaka kuhusianisha au kuhuisha
nyakati bali kujielewa zaidi na kutambua
mambo ambayo nililazimika kuvumilia.
yalikuwa mambo ambayo nilipaswa kuyajua
vizuri ili kuwafundisha watu wengine kuhusu
masomo ambayo nilipaswa kujifunza.

# SANAA-YA-UKWELI

Masomo hututayarisha kwa siku zijazo na ni funguo
muhimu kwa milango ambayo imefungwa.
Kuhifadhi hisia hizi ambazo hazihisiwi
vizuri huharibu tabia halisi ya wengi.
Kutamani majibu ya kwanini jambo fulani lilinitokea
ni hali ya kawaida ya jamii, ni sawa na kusema
"HABARI", badala ya kuingia ndani na kuomba
au kutafakari hali ili kupata ukweli na utambulisho
halisi wa kwa nini jambo fulani limetokea.
Mara moja niliacha kujisemea na kuanza kujisemea,
niliona mambo na kusikia mambo kwa uwazi zaidi.
Angalia unapozungumza na wewe mwenyewe,
utaendelea kukaa sawa na kujidanganya lakini
unapozungumza na wewe mwenyewe unakuwa
thabiti zaidi, mzuri, na wazi juu ya mipaka
yako ambayo inaleta mabadiliko unayotafuta
ili kuondokana na hisia mbichi za WHY me.

# SWALI-MBICHI-HEWA

Je, umekosa fursa ngapi kwa sababu

ya hisia zisizochujwa?

Je, umeondoa mahusiano mangapi yanayoweza

kutokea katika maisha yako bila kujua kwa

sababu ya hisia hizo zisizochujwa?

Je, ingekuwa ya kuvutia vipi KWAKO

kuwa huru hatimaye?

Je, uko tayari kuchimba kwa ajili ya kupona kwako?

Je, uko tayari kuishi katika ukweli wako

au (UONGO) nje ya ukweli wako?

# CHAPTER 8

## {Up}-Rooted & {Under}Developed

The transformation of who I was birthed

to be started where I (ENDED).

Experiencing mental and emotional

abuse from a noticeably early age is what

triggered my form of co-dependency and a

need to people please as I grew older

With having a father and a mother there

was still no function of proper LOVE

until I had gotten older in age.

With the damage already done. I had learned to block out all emotions and put on a mask 50% of the time and that stuck with me until my mid 20's.

I blamed my parents and others for my numbness to an extent before realizing that I could fix what was now fully my responsibility.

I realized that I never knew or asked how they were treated by family members, friends, and lovers to the point where they may have been traumatized coming up and covered up there emotional and mental states also.

It was hard to ask because I did not want to pry into something and trigger my mother, but I needed answers.

Just as I stated in a previous chapter the tree had been chopped down and it was long and mighty fall. Terror raced threw me because I did not know what to expect as I prayed and asked for guidance during my process.

Exploring the inner shift within my world I
had to finally face the ROOT head on.

I had to awaken the child that was inside of
me and told her that we had to talk about

I have been humbled many times before,
but this time was different now the student
really did meet the teacher and that was my
younger self because she was going to teach me
everything that I needed to know about me.

So, I sat with Candace and cried for everything she had to bare by picking up the scattered and broken pieces of her to reconfigure the truth. I had to identify SOUL-Y with her because of the fragileness of her wellbeing. Establishing one's true identity was the new layout and design with pure intentions to become the best version of her past-present and future self.

# ART-OF-FACT

Would you like to know why after all that you have done and sacrificed, you are still confused on why you are feeling depressed, anxious, scared, and scattered but have forgiven the past situations and individuals?

YOU HAVE FORGIVEN EVERYONE ELSE BUT (YOURSELF)

A major part of healing any form of your world is first forgive yourself.

I had accomplished many things in my life, and this was one of the greatest.

I was able to fully release and let go of everything that had hindered me and the things that no longer required my attention or

never should gotten my attention

To build and restore your own hope after being under construction embracing the new identity that was now purely made up of love, truth, and authenticity. Serving myself with nothing but kindness.

Now fully understanding the translations of not only my words but GOD's words because my pain has birthed an abundance of RAW beauty that rejuvenates others MIND, BODIES and SOULS.

PEOPLE WORK BETTER WHEN THEY KNOW WHAT THE GOAL IS AND WHY

-ELON MUSK-

# 3 8 1 16 20 5 18

## 21 16 18 15 15 20 5 4 21 14 4 5
## 18 4 5 22 5 12 15 16 5 4

20 8 5 20 18 1 14 19 6 15 18 13 1 20 9 15 14 15 6 23 8

15 9 23 1 19 2 9 18 20 8 5 4 20 15 2 5 19 20 1 18 20 5

4 23 8 5 18 5 9 5 14 4 5 4 5 24 16 5 18 9 5 14 3 9 14 7

13 5 14 20 1 12 1 14 4 5 13 15 20 9 15 14 1 12 1 2 21

19 5 6 18 15 13 1 14 15 20 9 3 5 1 2 12 25 5 1 18 12

25 1 7 5 9 19 23 8 1 20 20 18 9 7 7 5 18 5 4 13 25 6

15 18 13 15 6 3 15 4 5 16 5 14 4 5 14 3 25 1 14 4 1 14

5 5 4 20 15 16 5 15 16 12 5 16 12 5 1 19 5 1 19 9 7 18

5 23 15 12 4 5 18 23 9 20 8 8 1 22 9 14 7 1 6 1 20 8 5

18 1 14 4 1 13 15 20 8 5 18 20 8 5 18 5 23 1 19 19 20

9 12 12 14 15 6 21 14 3 20 9 15 14 15 6 16 18 15 16 5

18 12 15 22 5 21 14 20 9 12 9 8 1 4 7 15 20 20 5 14 15

12 4 5 18 9 14 1 7 5 23 9 20 8 20 8 5 4 1 13 1 7 5 1 12

18 5 1 4 25 4 15 14 5 9 8 1 4 12 5 1 18 14 5 4 20 15 2

12 15 3 11 15 21 20 1 12 12 5 13 15 20 9 15 14 19 1 14
4 16 21 20 15 14 1 13 1 19 11 15 6 20 8 5 20 9 13 5 1
14 4 20 8 1 20 19 20 21 3 11 23 9 20 8 13 5 21 14 20 9
12 13 25 13 9 4 19 9 2 12 1 13 5 4 13 25 16 1 18 5 14
20 19 1 14 4 15 20 8 5 18 19 6 15 18 13 25 14 21 13 2
14 5 19 19 20 15 1 14 5 24 20 5 14 20 2 5 6 15 18 5 18
5 1 12 9 26 9 14 7 20 8 1 20 9 3 15 21 12 4 6 9 24 23
8 1 20 23 1 19 14 15 23 6 21 12 12 25 13 25 18 5 19
16 15 14 19 9 2 9 12 9 20 25 9 18 5 1 12 9 26 5 4 20 8
1 20 9 14 5 22 5 18 11 14 5 23 15 18 1 19 11 5 4 8 15
23 20 8 5 25 23 5 18 5 20 18 5 1 20 5 4 2 25 6 1 13 9
12 25 13 5 13 2 5 18 19 6 18 9 5 14 4 19 1 14 4 12 15
22 5 18 19 20 15 20 8 5 16 15 9 14 20 23 8 5 18 5 20
8 5 25 13 1 25 8 1 22 5 2 5 5 14 20 18 1 21 13 1 20 9
26 5 4 3 15 13 9 14 7 21 16 1 14 4 3 15 22 5 18 5 4 21
16 20 8 5 18 5 5 13 15 20 9 15 14 1 12 1 14 4 13 5 14
20 1 12 19 20 1 20 5 19 1 12 19 15 9 20 23 1 19 8 1 18
4 20 15 1 19 11 2 5 3 1 21 19 5 9 4 9 4 14 15 20 23 1

14 20 20 15 16 18 25 9 14 20 15 19 15 13 5 20 8 9 14

7 1 14 4 20 18 9 7 7 5 18 13 25 13 15 20 8 5 18 2 21

20 9 14 5 5 4 5 4 1 14 19 23 5 18 19 10 21 19 20 1 19

9 19 20 1 20 5 4 9 14 1 16 18 5 22 9 15 21 19 3 8 1 16

20 5 18 20 8 5 20 18 5 5 8 1 4 2 5 5 14 3 8 15 16 16 5

4 4 15 23 14 1 14 4 9 20 23 1 19 12 15 14 7 1 14 4 13

9 7 8 20 25 6 1 12 12 20 5 18 18 15 18 18 1 3 5 4 20 8

18 5 23 13 5 2 5 3 1 21 19 5 9 4 9 4 14 15 20 11 14 15

23 23 8 1 20 20 15 5 24 16 5 3 20 1 19 9 16 18 1 25 5

4 1 14 4 1 19 11 5 4 6 15 18 7 21 9 4 1 14 3 5 4 21 18

9 14 7 13 25 16 18 15 3 5 19 19 5 24 16 12 15 18 9 14

7 20 8 5 9 14 14 5 18 19 8 9 6 20 23 9 20 8 9 14 13 25

23 15 18 12 4 9 8 1 4 20 15 6 9 14 1 12 12 25 6 1 3 5

20 8 5 18 15 15 20 8 5 1 4 15 14 9 8 1 4 20 15 1 23 1

11 5 14 20 8 5 3 8 9 12 4 20 8 1 20 23 1 19 9 14 19 9

4 5 15 6 13 5 1 14 4 20 15 12 4 8 5 18 20 8 1 20 23 5

8 1 4 20 15 20 1 12 11 1 2 15 21 20 9 8 1 22 5 2 5 5

14 8 21 13 2 12 5 4 13 1 14 25 20 9 13 5 19 2 5 6 15

18 5 2 21 20 20 8 9 19 20 9 13 5 23 1 19 4 9 6 6 5 18
5 14 20 14 15 23 20 8 5 19 20 21 4 5 14 20 18 5 1 12
12 25 4 9 4 13 5 5 20 20 8 5 20 5 1 3 8 5 18 1 14 4 20
8 1 20 23 1 19 13 25 25 15 21 14 7 5 18 19 5 12 6 2 5
3 1 21 19 5 19 8 5 23 1 19 7 15 9 14 7 20 15 20 5 1 3
8 13 5 5 22 5 18 25 20 8 9 14 7 20 8 1 20 9 14 5 5 4 5
4 20 15 11 14 15 23 1 2 15 21 20 13 5 19 15 9 19 1 20
23 9 20 8 13 25 19 5 12 6 1 14 4 3 18 9 5 4 6 15 18 5
22 5 18 25 20 8 9 14 7 9 8 1 4 20 15 2 1 18 5 2 25 16
9 3 11 9 14 7 21 16 20 8 5 19 3 1 20 20 5 18 5 4 1 14
4 2 18 15 11 5 14 16 9 5 3 5 19 15 6 8 5 18 20 15 18 5
3 15 14 6 9 7 21 18 5 20 8 5 20 18 21 20 8 9 8 1 4 20
15 9 4 5 14 20 9 6 25 19 15 21 12 25 23 9 20 8 8 5 18
2 5 3 1 21 19 5 15 6 20 8 5 6 18 1 7 9 12 5 14 5 19 19
15 6 8 5 18 23 5 12 12 2 5 9 14 7 5 19 20 1 2 12 9 19
8 9 14 7 15 14 5 19 20 18 21 5 9 4 5 14 20 9 20 25 23
1 19 20 8 5 14 5 23 12 1 25 15 21 20 1 14 4 4 5 19 9 7
14 23 9 20 8 16 21 18 5 9 14 20 5 14 20 9 15 14 19 20

15 2 5 3 15 13 5 20 8 5 2 5 19 20 22 5 18 19 9 15 14

15 6 8 5 18 16 1 19 20 16 18 5 19 5 14 20 1 14 4 6 21

20 21 18 5 19 5 12 6 1 18 20 15 6 6 1 3 20 23 15 21 12

4 25 15 21 12 9 11 5 20 15 11 14 15 23 23 8 25 1 6 20

5 18 1 12 12 20 8 1 20 25 15 21 8 1 22 5 4 15 14 5 1

14 4 19 1 3 18 9 6 9 3 5 4 25 15 21 1 18 5 19 20 9 12

12 3 15 14 6 21 19 5 4 15 14 23 8 25 25 15 21 1 18 5 6

5 5 12 9 14 7 4 5 16 18 5 19 19 5 4 1 14 24 9 15 21 19

19 3 1 18 5 4 1 14 4 19 3 1 20 20 5 18 5 4 2 21 20 8 1

22 5 6 15 18 7 9 22 5 14 20 8 5 16 1 19 20 19 9 20 21

1 20 9 15 14 19 1 14 4 9 14 4 9 22 9 4 21 1 12 19 25

15 21 8 1 22 5 6 15 18 7 9 22 5 14 5 22 5 18 25 15 14

5 5 12 19 5 2 21 20 25 15 21 18 19 5 12 6 1 13 1 10 15

18 16 1 18 20 15 6 8 5 1 12 9 14 7 1 14 25 6 15 18 13

15 6 25 15 21 18 23 15 18 12 4 9 19 6 9 18 19 20 6 15

18 7 9 22 5 25 15 21 18 19 5 12 6 9 8 1 4 1 3 3 15 13

16 12 9 19 8 5 4 13 1 14 25 20 8 9 14 7 19 9 14 13 25

12 9 6 5 1 14 4 20 8 9 19 23 1 19 15 14 5 15 6 20 8 5

7 18 5 1 20 5 19 20 9 23 1 19 1 2 12 5 20 15 6 21 12
12 25 18 5 12 5 1 19 5 1 14 4 12 5 20 7 15 15 6 5 22 5
18 25 20 8 9 14 7 20 8 1 20 8 1 4 8 9 14 4 5 18 5 4 13
5 1 14 4 20 8 5 20 8 9 14 7 19 20 8 1 20 14 15 12 15
14 7 5 18 18 5 17 21 9 18 5 4 13 25 1 20 20 5 14 20 9
15 14 15 18 14 5 22 5 18 19 8 15 21 12 4 7 15 20 20 5
14 13 25 1 20 20 5 14 20 9 15 14 20 15 2 21 9 12 4 1
14 4 18 5 19 20 15 18 5 25 15 21 18 15 23 14 8 15 16
5 1 6 20 5 18 2 5 9 14 7 21 14 4 5 18 3 15 14 19 20 18
21 3 20 9 15 14 5 13 2 18 1 3 9 14 7 20 8 5 14 5 23 9
4 5 14 20 9 20 25 20 8 1 20 23 1 19 14 15 23 16 21 18
5 12 25 13 1 4 5 21 16 15 6 12 15 22 5 20 18 21 20 8
1 14 4 1 21 20 8 5 14 20 9 3 9 20 25 19 5 18 22 9 14 7
13 25 19 5 12 6 23 9 20 8 14 15 20 8 9 14 7 2 21 20 11
9 14 4 14 5 19 19 14 15 23 6 21 12 12 25 21 14 4 5 18
19 20 1 14 4 9 14 7 20 8 5 20 18 1 14 19 12 1 20 9 15
14 19 15 6 14 15 20 15 14 12 25 13 25 23 15 18 4 19 2
21 20 7 15 4 19 23 15 18 4 19 2 5 3 1 21 19 5 13 25 16

1 9 14 8 1 19 2 9 18 20 8 5 4 1 14 1 2 21 14 4 1 14 3 5

15 6 18 1 23 2 5 1 21 20 25 20 8 1 20 18 5 10 21 22 5

14 1 20 5 19 15 20 8 5 18 19 13 9 14 4 2 15 4 9 5 19 1

14 4 19 15 21 12 19 16 5 15 16 12 5 23 15 18 11 2 5 20

20 5 18 23 8 5 14 20 8 5 25 11 14 15 23 23 8 1 20 20 8

5 7 15 1 12 9 19 1 14 4 23 8 25 5 12 15 14 13 21 19 11

# CHAPTER 9

## To You, From Me:

How would you decipher to discover

"YOUR TRUTH"?

Are you feeling about your own

Vibrational Frequency?

Why are you more vulnerable to

others than "YOUR-SELF"?

What / Who does "YOUR" ROOT look like?

Why do you keep climbing the same

mountain that was removed for you?

# CHAPTER 10

## Live In Your Truth

Who are "YOU"?

If "YOU" know that time is a thief, why do "YOU" give it to things/ people that have no meaning?

What things have "YOU" mastered in your life that are of substance for your life?

Are "YOU" releasing or re-leasing?

After sorting out the REAL "YOU" what do you plan to do with HIM/HER?

# CHAPTER 11

## The Cost

All I needed was for one person to believe in me and when (I) finally did realizing that I never needed anyone else's YES to go forward and thrive, once I realized everything that I had encountered and had accomplished beating and cheating death as well as mental and emotional abuse I was actually going to make "time "stand still for me.

I cannot change what has transpired in my life but what I will do is never jeopardize my character, morals, and integrity again, holding them to highest standards to make sure that others would not have to endure what I went through.

# ART-OF-FACT

MAKE SURE YOU KNOW ALL OF THE

LYRICS TO YOUR OWN SONG BEFORE

YOU LEARN SOMEONE ELSES

-WORDPLAY BEAUTY-

It is the help that I didn't get that helped me the most

-KING NIPSEY HUSSLE-

As tall as a Sequoias tree

My roots buried deep in the Ethers

My heart carved in the bark

My back arched as the leaves are

placed elegantly upon me

Hair being kissed by the wind

My uncanny beauty being seen as I let the Sun rays in

The person I once was

I left her in the shadows with fear

The woman that stands before you

Unbothered and Basking in Glorious Tears

-ROOTING for YOU,

-WORDPLAY BEAUTY-

I TRULY LOVE EACH AND EVERYONE OF YOU; I THANK YOU FOR YOUR SUPPORT

Printed in the United States
by Baker & Taylor Publisher Services